SPACE UNIVERSITY™

THE SPACE EXPLORER'S GUIDE TO the Universe

BY **BILL DOYLE**

WITH **RACHEL CONNOLLY**
SPACE EDUCATOR

RYAN WYATT
VISUAL ADVISOR

AND **JIM SWEITZER**, PH.D.
NASA SCIENCE CENTER,
DePAUL UNIVERSITY

SCHOLASTIC INC.

NEW YORK   TORONTO   LONDON   AUCKLAND   SYDNEY
MEXICO CITY   NEW DELHI   HONG KONG   BUENOS AIRES

W9-DHN-661

Who's Who at Space U

Bill Doyle
Writer

Bill is a writer who lives in New York City. He has written for Sesame Workshop, TIME For Kids, the Discovery Channel, LeapFrog, and the American Museum of Natural History.

Rachel Connolly
Consultant

Rachel manages the astrophysics education program at the American Museum of Natural History's Rose Center for Earth and Space.

Ryan Wyatt
Visual Advisor

Ryan designs scientific visuals for the American Museum of Natural History's Rose Center for Earth and Space.

Jim Sweitzer
Advisor

Jim is an astrophysicist and the director of the NASA Space Science Center at DePaul University in Chicago.

ISBN: 0-439-55739-9

Copyright © 2003 by Scholastic Inc.

Editor: Andrea Menotti
Designers: Lee Kaplan, Peggy Gardner
Cover designer: Mark Neston
Illustrators: Yancey C. Labat, Thomas Nackid, Ed Shems

Front cover: Earth from orbit (image by NASA).
Back cover: The spiral galaxy known as M-109 (image by NOAO/AURA/NSF).

Page 4, top: NASA/JPL. Page 5, bottom: NASA/JPL/USGS. Page 8: (Galileo) Sheila Terry/Photo Researchers, (Payne) Kathy Haramundanis. Page 9 (all): NASA. Pages 10, 11, and 46 (top): R. Stöckli/Robert Simmon/NASA GSFC/MODIS. Page 11, top: (Mercury) NASA/JPL/Northwestern, (Venus) NASA/Pioneer Venus, (Mars) NASA/STScI/Colorado/Cornell/SSI, (Jupiter) NASA/JPL/USGS, (Saturn, Uranus, and Neptune) NASA/JPL, (Pluto) NASA/ESA/SWRI/Lowell Observatory. Page 11, bottom: European Southern Observatory. Pages 12–13: Axel Mellinger. Page 13, bottom: Jerry Schad/Photo Researchers. Page 14: AP/Wide World. Page 17: (astronaut) NASA/Jim Ross, (shuttle) NASA, (Saturn) NASA/JPL, (Jupiter) NASA/JPL/USGS, (Earth) NASA, (supernova) Gallagher (U. Wisconsin)/WIYN/NOAO/NSF, (nebula) Sharp/NOAO/AURA/NSF. Page 18: (irregular galaxy) NASA/ESA/Hubble Heritage Team (STScI/AURA), (spiral galaxy) Todd Boroson/NOAO/AURA/NSF, (Hubble Deep Field) Robert Williams and the Hubble Deep Field Team (STScI) and NASA. Page 23: (top) NASA, (bottom) Courtesy of Meade Telescopes. Page 29: NASA/JPL-Caltech, courtesy of Dr. Michelle Thaller. Pages 31–35: All images and patches by NASA. Page 38 (all): NASA. Page 45 (all): NASA/JPL. Page 46, bottom: NASA artwork. Page 47: Roeland P. van der Marel (STScI)/Frank C. van den Bosch (U. Washington)/NASA.

12 11 10 9 8 7 6 5 4   6 7 8/0

Printed in the U.S.A.

First Scholastic printing, October 2003

The publisher has made every effort to ensure that the activities in this book are safe when done as instructed. Adults should provide guidance and supervision whenever the activity requires.

Table of Contents

Welcome to

Greetings, Earthling! Have you ever looked up at the night sky and wondered, "What's out there?" Or, "*Who's* out there?" Or, "What would it be like to *travel* out there?" Or...

Does the universe go on *forever*?

How much of the universe can we see?

What would happen if I fell into a black hole?

What do astronauts eat in space?

How do astronauts go to the bathroom in space?

Is there life on Mars?

How hot is the Sun?

When was the Earth born?

When was the *universe* born?

What was there *before* the universe?

Why do stars twinkle?

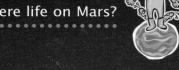
Why is space black?

What keeps stuff on Earth from flying off into space?

How can *I* get into space?

Space University!

Well, you've come to the right place to find out the answers to all of your cosmic questions. This is Space University—where you can become a totally out-of-this-world space explorer! Start the countdown, because you're about to launch yourself into the last great frontier: space!

SPACE WHO? SPACE U!

This university is truly a *universe*-ity! As a Space U student—or "cadet," as we'll call you—you'll learn how the universe works, what's in it, what *might* be in it, and how you (as in U!) can join in the discovery. By the time you accomplish your final mission at Space U, you'll be a fully certified space explorer, ready for whatever you encounter in this galaxy—or the next!

WHAT'S THIS BOOK ALL ABOUT?

This handbook is the launching pad for your intergalactic journey. It's fully stocked with everything you need to get started on your cosmic quest to become a space explorer. Then, each month after this, for as long as you stay on the Space U crew, you'll get another book that focuses in depth on one part of the space frontier.

As you probe the pages of this space program, you'll discover:

MISSIONS AND QUICK BLASTS

Space U Mission Control has crammed this book full of fun missions that will expand your smarts about space. You'll launch a mini-rocket, send a marshmallow on a space walk (without a space suit!), create your own galaxies—and much more! You'll also find lots of Quick Blasts scattered around these pages. These are mini-missions designed to keep Space U cadets' brains bubbling.

ASTROTALES

These are stories of real-life space adventures, discoveries, and mysteries. Zap back in time and find out how we've made it so far in our space explorations, and meet the people who helped us take our biggest strides.

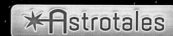

MEET THE STARS

Throughout your course of study, Space U will introduce you to all sorts of astronauts and space scientists who are working right now to expand our understanding of the universe. They'll give you the inside scoop on what it means to have your head in the stars!

FLASH FACTS

Quick and fast—just right for cadets on the go— this cool-to-know space info is beamed in directly from Mission Control.

THE SPACE UNIVERSITY WEB SITE

To keep you plugged in at all times, Space University *also* has a home in cyberspace at www.scholastic.com/space. This fun-packed web site was created especially for Space U cadets, and it's fully loaded with great space challenges and games. Make sure to visit soon! But don't forget the secret password (which you can find below on Planet Password), because only Space U cadets have authorization to enter the site!

And get this: Each month, when you receive your new book, you'll be given clearance to enter the next level of the Space U web site with a new password. You'll find your new password right here each month on Planet Password.

PLANET PASSWORD
This month's web site password is:
GOSPACE

When you complete all the challenges and games on the Space U web site, you can print out your personalized mission patch and paste it here. (If you're wondering what a mission patch is, check out page 33!)

If you think one of the coolest things about becoming a space explorer is the number of space-age gizmos you get—you're right! Here's what's in your Space Case this month:

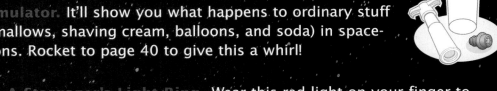

- **A Space Simulator.** It'll show you what happens to ordinary stuff (like marshmallows, shaving cream, balloons, and soda) in space-like conditions. Rocket to page 40 to give this a whirl!

- **A Stargazer's Light Ring.** Wear this red light on your finger to help you jot down notes while you're checking out the stars. It won't ruin your night vision like regular flashlights will. Flash over to page 26 to shed light on this subject!

- **Glow-in-the-Dark Stars.** Sure, you're *already* a star, but here are more stars to shine around you. And guess what—these stars come in colors, just like real stars do. Stick 'em up and create constellations or design your own galaxy. *Glow* on over to page 27 to try 'em out!

Did you know that stars come in colors? They do! They come in red, orange, yellow, white, and blue. The colors depend on the star's temperature—red are the coolest, blue are the hottest, and the other colors are in between. The stars might all *look* white when you see them outside at night, but let your eyes get used to the dark, and you might start to see some colors!

- **Team Universe Cards.** Get to know the stars and other major players that make the universe such a winning team. Flip to page 19 to see how they stack up!

- **A Space University Mission Patch.** Stick this on your notebook (or wear it on your space suit!) to show your Space U school spirit. See page 33 to get patched in!

- **A Space Case.** If you're wondering where on *Earth* you're going to store all your space supplies, here's your answer!

Don't Space Out!

Mission Control will alert you when missions require extra personnel or an IGA (Intergalactic Adult). It's a Space U rule: Before you launch these activities, you must include an adult in your mission plan. All Space U cadets are expected to run a tight ship—a tight *space* ship, that is!

the BIGThree

Space is a huge place! So Mission Control will divide your space program into three major categories: **astronomy**, **astrophysics**, and **space exploration**.

ASTRONOMY

Anyone can do it! The oldest science, astronomy began thousands of years ago, long before there were telescopes. People simply looked up at the stars, started naming them— and astronomy was born! The word "astronomy" actually means "name the stars," but that's just *one* of the things astronomers do. This field is all about observing and recording the locations and movements of space objects, like stars and planets.

✴Astrotales

Why'd the World Go Ga-Ga Over Galileo?

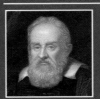

In 1610 (that's four hundred years ago!), Italian astronomer Galileo Galilei found spots on the Sun, craters on the Moon, and four (of the many) moons of Jupiter. He discovered all of this using a great new telescope he'd designed and built himself— a device that was far more powerful than other telescopes available at the time.

ASTROPHYSICS

Astrophysics is one of the youngest sciences. It goes a step beyond astronomy and explores how objects in space (like stars, galaxies, black holes—you name it!) are made, what they're made of, and how they interact with each other. A field for smarties (like you!), astrophysics was born when we put prisms on telescopes and started to see the spectra (or colors) of the stars. Seeing these colors helped us learn what stars are made of.

Light beam

A prism bends light and breaks it up into a spectrum of color.

✴Astrotales

No Payne, No Gain!

That's the way many astrophysicists feel about Cecilia Payne (1900–1979), one of the founders of their science. Payne answered a big question that led to the birth of astrophysics: *What are stars made of?* Payne showed us that stars are made from the same stuff you find here on Earth, including helium (like the kind that fills balloons), oxygen (which you breathe), and hydrogen (one of the building blocks of water).

SPACE EXPLORATION

The exploration of space is about traveling beyond our planet's atmosphere. As you can probably guess, this is the part of Space U where the astronauts hang out! Here you'll find rockets, shuttles, and space stations, as well as unmanned probes that make long journeys to far-out places like Mars, Jupiter, Saturn, and beyond—and beam information back to scientists on Earth.

Space agencies around the world (like NASA, which you'll read about on page 31) have the resources to launch all kinds of knowledge-expanding missions into space. The stuff we learn on these missions helps us understand our world, unravel the mysteries of the universe, and advance the technology that can improve our lives on Earth. And, of course, the more we learn, the farther we can go. Where to next, cadet?

✳Astrotales

Fly Me to the Moon!

In 1969, the commander of NASA's *Apollo 11* mission, Neil Armstrong, became the first human to set foot on the Moon. He did so with these words: "That's one small step for man, one giant leap for mankind." It was the first time any human had ever stood on a celestial body other than Earth!

Well, Armstrong may have been the first to walk on the Moon, but (cadet, put your name here) might be the first to visit Mars! That's right—a human footprint on the dusty red surface of Mars is entirely possible in the not-so-distant future. Will it be yours?

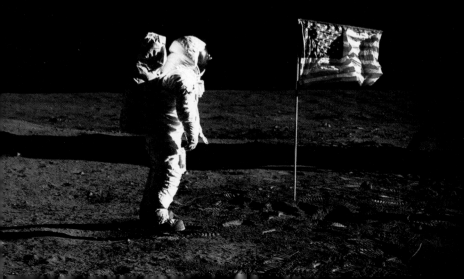

Astronaut Buzz Aldrin, on the *Apollo 11* mission in 1969, walking on the surface of the Moon.

Ready for the first stop on your tour of the universe? Then turn the page and find out *where* we are in the universe, and *when* we are in the history of time!

9 <<

Where are we in space, and when are we in time? Good question, cadet! Let's start with the *where* part first.

GIVE ME SOME SPACE!

Space is almost totally empty of matter. Sure, you've got *clumps* of matter (like planets and stars), but in between these clumps there really isn't much at all—just bits of cosmic dust and particles scattered here and there.

FLASH FACT

"Matter" is another word for "stuff." Everything in the universe (including you!) is made up of matter. The "mass" of an object is the amount of matter it has in it.

In the midst of this rather unpleasant, dark, empty place spins a lovely place we call home, Earth. (Insert pleasant sigh here.) Our little planet circles a star called the Sun. And while we want to *think* we have the biggest, baddest star around, the Sun is just average compared to other stars, and it's just one of 200 billion stars in our spiral-shaped, spinning galaxy, the Milky Way.

Can you spot home sweet home—otherwise known as Earth—on this map of our solar system? (Hint: Look for the third rock from the Sun!)

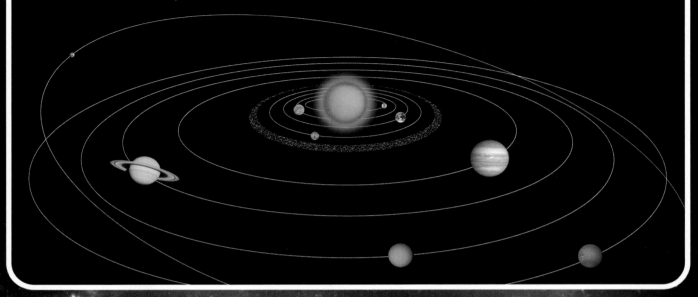

ZOOM OUT EVEN FARTHER...

Here's a picture of how we *think* our Milky Way galaxy looks from outside (since we've never been outside our galaxy, we don't have any snapshots!). The circle marks the location of our solar system.

YOU ARE HERE

WHAT'S BEYOND?

Our galaxy is just one of *billions* in the universe!

Want to see the Milky Way as we see it from Earth? You don't have to wait for nightfall—as a Space U cadet, you can view the galaxy anytime you want, 24 hours a day! Just turn the page....

Here you have it: The enormous Milky Way galaxy, as seen from Earth.

To create this image, a German astro-photographer named Axel Mellinger traveled around the world for three years (from 1996 to 1999) to take pictures of the night sky, using special camera techniques to capture more starlight than our eyes can take in. Then he used a computer to stitch the photos together. The result is an image that shows you much more of the galaxy than you'd ever see in a night of stargazing on your part of the planet. Try the Quick Blast below to get better acquainted with the whole wide Milky Way!

QuickBlast

Star Search!

Take a quick tour around our galaxy. Can you spot the following star attractions? You can check your answers on page 48.

BETELGEUSE

RIGEL

A. Orion. This is a constellation known as the Hunter. You can see a red star called Betelgeuse (pronounced "Beetlejuice") and a blue star called Rigel (RYE-jul) in this constellation.

B. Andromeda Galaxy. The Andromeda galaxy is one of the Milky Way's neighbor galaxies. It's really far away, so it looks like a tiny smudge—but there are billions of stars packed in there! Our galaxy would look a lot like this one if viewed from far away.

C. The Large Magellanic Cloud. This is another galaxy! It's our closest neighbor galaxy, but it's not a very big one (our Milky Way is about twenty times bigger!). It's visible in the Earth's Southern Hemisphere.

D. The Small Magellanic Cloud. This is yet *another* neighbor galaxy. It's really small, only a quarter of the size of its nearby companion, the Large Magellanic Cloud. The two "clouds" got their names from the Portuguese explorer Ferdinand Magellan, who sailed to the Southern Hemisphere in 1519 and noticed these galaxies in the night sky. He thought they looked like little clouds.

WHY DOES IT LOOK THIS WAY?

Because our galaxy is a thin disk, and because we're inside it, the Milky Way looks like a band of stars to us. See the bright yellow part in the center? That's the core of the galaxy, a glowing region of heated dust and gas. The white cloudy streaks across the middle are made up of billions of stars that are so far away (and appear so close together), they all get blurred into a haze. The black cloudy streaks are regions full of cosmic dust that blocks the starlight. The stars are the usual ones you see—you just don't normally see so many of them at once!

FLASH FACT

How did the Milky Way get its name? (No, there aren't any space cows—that's "udderly" ridiculous!) About 2,500 years ago, ancient Greeks thought the Milky Way looked like a pool of milk that a goddess had spilled across the sky. They called the galaxy *Kiklos Galaxias*—or Milky Circle. The ancient Romans called it *Via Lactea* (Latin for "Milky Way").

Here's what the cloudy white streaks of the Milky Way look like on a dark, clear night in the country. Can you see how the Milky Way got its name?

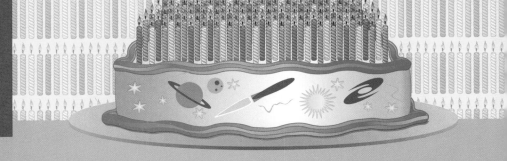

Where are we in space, and when are we in time? We've talked about the *where* part of this question... Now let's move on to the *when* part!

Happy 13.7 Billionth Birthday, UNIVERSE!

Imagine trying to blow out 13,700,000,000 (that's 13.7 *billion*) candles! Well, that's about how many you'd have to extinguish if you were the universe celebrating your birthday. The universe burst onto the scene about 13.7 billion years ago with the Big Bang, the monumental event that created space and time and all the matter and energy in the entire universe (whoa!). Our Sun and the planets that go around the Sun (including the Earth) are just babies in comparison...only about 4.6 billion years old!

FLASH FACT

13.7 billion is the short way of writing 13 billion plus 700 million! That's a huuuuuge number! To get 13.7 billion candles on a birthday cake for the universe, you'd need a cake the size of fifty football fields!

DAYS DAZE

Cadet, meet Carl Sagan. He was a great astrophysicist who did something really cool with calendars. He said that we should think about the history of the universe as if it were one calendar year, starting on January 1 with the Big Bang and ending on December 31 with the present day. Get this—on Sagan's calendar, humans (like you!) wouldn't appear until about 11:00 p.m. on December 31! We haven't been around very long, have we?

Carl Sagan (1934–1996)

Here's how the cosmic calendar works:
- Each day on the calendar represents 37.5 million years.
- Each hour is equal to 1.5 million years.
- Each minute is 26,048 years.
- And each second is 434 years!

QuickBlast

Mark your calendar!

Where do you think the birth of the Sun and the formation of the Earth would fall on the cosmic calendar? You can check your answer on page 48!

Cosmic Calendar

Jan. 1

BIG BANG

Feb. 14–Mar. 12
Galaxies form

JANUARY
S	M	T	W	T	F	S
			1	2	3	
4	5	6	7	8	9	10
11	12	13	14	15	16	17
18	19	20	21	22	23	24
25	26	27	28	29	30	31

FEBRUARY
S	M	T	W	T	F	S
1	2	3	4	5	6	7
8	9	10	11	12	13	14
15	16	17	18	19	20	21
22	23	24	25	26	27	28
29						

MARCH
S	M	T	W	T	F	S
1	2	3	4	5	6	
7	8	9	10	11	12	13
14	15	16	17	18	19	20
21	22	23	24	25	26	27
28	29	30	31			

APRIL
S	M	T	W	T	F	S
				1	2	3
4	5	6	7	8	9	10
11	12	13	14	15	16	17
18	19	20	21	22	23	24
25	26	27	28	29	30	

MAY
S	M	T	W	T	F	S
						1
2	3	4	5	6	7	8
9	10	11	12	13	14	15
16	17	18	19	20	21	22
23	24	25	26	27	28	29
30	31					

JUNE
S	M	T	W	T	F	S
	1	2	3	4	5	
6	7	8	9	10	11	12
13	14	15	16	17	18	19
20	21	22	23	24	25	26
27	28	29	30			

JULY
S	M	T	W	T	F	S
				1	2	3
4	5	6	7	8	9	10
11	12	13	14	15	16	17
18	19	20	21	22	23	24
25	26	27	28	29	30	31

AUGUST
S	M	T	W	T	F	S
1	2	3	4	5	6	7
8	9	10	11	12	13	14
15	16	17	18	19	20	21
22	23	24	25	26	27	28
29	30	31				

SEPTEMBER
S	M	T	W	T	F	S
		1	2	3	4	
5	6	7	8	9	10	11
12	13	14	15	16	17	18
19	20	21	22	23	24	25
26	27	28	29	30		

OCTOBER
S	M	T	W	T	F	S
					1	2
3	4	5	6	7	8	9
10	11	12	13	14	15	16
17	18	19	20	21	22	23
24	25	26	27	28	29	30
31						

NOVEMBER
S	M	T	W	T	F	S
	1	2	3	4	5	6
7	8	9	10	11	12	13
14	15	16	17	18	19	20
21	22	23	24	25	26	27
28	29	30				

DECEMBER
S	M	T	W	T	F	S
		1	2	3	4	
5	6	7	8	9	10	11
12	13	14	15	16	17	18
19	20	21	22	23	24	25
26	27	28	29	30	31	

Sept. 19
The first forms of life appear in Earth's oceans

Dec. 31, 11:00 p.m.
The first humans appear!

QuickBlast

Your Body of Knowledge!

Want to share your smarts about the history of the universe? Then round up an audience and try this!

1 Stand near a wall and hold out your arms on either side of you, with your index fingers pointing out.

2 Explain to the audience that your arms represent the cosmic timeline. One fingertip is the starting point, the Big Bang, and the other fingertip is the present day. The distance from one fingertip to the other fingertip represents the entire 13.7-billion-year history of the universe. Allow a few seconds for this information to sink in.

3 Ask, "Where do you think human history falls on this timeline?" Let the audience guess.

BEGINNING OF TIME

PRESENT DAY

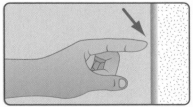

4 Rub the "present-day" fingertip lightly against the wall. Explain that you just rubbed away the very, very tip of your fingernail, and when you did that, you wiped out the entire history of the human race! That's how short of a time we've been around!

5 After the "oohs" and "ahhs" have diminished, drop your arms and take a bow!

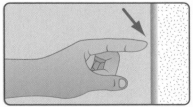

Part 2:
Try This On For Size!

As you rocket through the universe, you'll be exploring all sorts of objects—from the unimaginably immense to the tiniest of the tiny. It can be mind-melting enough to make *anyone's* thrusters backfire! To keep things moving along, the super minds of Space U have broken down the different sizes into the six scales—or measurement categories—that you'll find below. Just remember, not everything fits neatly into one of these categories, and there aren't any solid lines dividing the scales.

THE SIZE SCALES OF THE UNIVERSE

ATOMIC   HUMAN   PLANETARY   STELLAR   GALACTIC   UNIVERSAL

ATOMIC SCALE

Don't bother squinting, cadet! Things here, like protons, neutrons, and electrons, are so *micro* that you'll never see them with your naked eyes. Objects in this scale are the building blocks that make up all the stuff in every other scale. When you put protons, neutrons, and electrons in different combinations, you get atoms. When you put atoms together, you get molecules that combine to make cells, people, animals, Space U cadets, and everything else you can think of (including brussel sprouts and anchovies).

But wait! We haven't told you about the *tiniest* guys. Protons and neutrons are actually made up of even smaller particles called quarks.

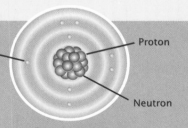

Electron — Proton

Neutron

Oxygen atom

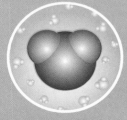

Water molecule

HUMAN SCALE

This is all the stuff that we can touch and interact with—like other people, cars, spaceships, aardvarks, kumquats, spotted garden slugs—you know, the everyday stuff! The things in this scale (and every scale after this one) are all made up of atoms. Did you know it takes as many atoms as there are grains of sand on Earth to make *one* human being?

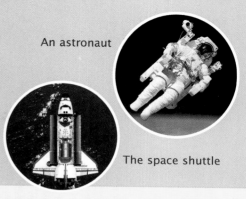

An astronaut

The space shuttle

PLANETARY SCALE

A lot more than planets are found in this scale. Take your pick of moons, large comets, and asteroids. Like all the other scales, there's no specific definition of what's here, but these objects are all larger than the largest mountains on our home world.

Not sure if something belongs in the scale? Give it the Space U Stick Test: If it's floating in space and you stick to it (thanks to its gravity), the object belongs here.

Saturn

Jupiter

Earth

STELLAR SCALE

Close your eyes, cadet. Now, imagine.... Wait a second, you can't read with your eyes closed! Okay, let's try this again.

Keep your eyes open. Now, imagine that you have more mass than a planet. Your gravity is strong enough to squeeze you together very tightly. The closer your atoms get squeezed together, the hotter you get—until you get hot enough to glow with your own visible light. Now, you're really a *star*!

Besides stars, what else is in this scale? All the objects that are involved in the life cycle of a star, like the places where baby stars are born—star-forming nebulae; and the various ways that a star can die. A star can go out with a *bang*, in an explosion called a supernova that collapses into a pulsar or a black hole—or it can swell out into a cloud of dust called a planetary nebula.

A supernova

A star-forming nebula

FLASH FACT

Gravity is the force of attraction between objects. The more mass an object has, the more strongly it pulls other objects toward it. Earth's gravity pulls on objects (like you!) and holds them on its surface. More massive objects like big planets or stars have even stronger forces of gravity.

An irregular galaxy

A spiral galaxy

GALACTIC SCALE

You guessed it, cadet: Galaxies like the Milky Way are in this scale. They're made up of billions of stars held together by gravity. Galaxies can have different sizes and shapes, such as spiral (like our Milky Way) or elliptical (oval-shaped).

The galactic scale also contains quasars—the powerful centers of young, distant galaxies that emit radio waves, X rays, and other forms of light.

UNIVERSAL SCALE

The *universe* belongs in this scale! It's so huge that no one can claim to know everything that's in it. All the stuff that we can detect with our telescopes and other tools is what we call the observable universe. But there is so much that we can't see! How much? Who knows! We might be able to observe only a *fraction* of the entire universe!

What we can see in this scale are groupings of galaxies that we call superclusters and big bubbles of seemingly empty space. The boundary of our neck of the universe is the leftover energy from the Big Bang itself, called the Cosmic Microwave Background Radiation (not the most poetic name, right?). This energy forms the very edge of our observable universe.

This image, created by the Hubble Space Telescope, shows *hundreds* of galaxies!

SIZE 'EM UP!

Okay, cadet, you've read about all the different sizes of things in the universe, including the universe itself! But do you really know your stuff?

Launch Objective

▷ **Figure out how the Team Universe players stack up against each other with these two cosmically entertaining games.**

Your equipment

▶ **Team Universe cards** SPACE Case
▶ **Six pieces of paper**
▶ **Pencil**

Personnel

▶ **A friend to play with (for Size Prize)**

Mission Procedure

Part 1: Place Your Order

1 On each sheet of paper, write the name of one size scale: Atomic, Human, Planetary, Stellar, Galactic, or Universal. Line up the papers in a row from the smallest scale to the largest scale.

2 Shuffle your Team Universe cards so they're all mixed up.

3 Now, using what you learned about scales on pages 16–18, place each card on a sheet of paper in the size scale where it belongs.

4 How do you know if you got everything in the right scale? Turn to page 48 to find out!

ATOMIC

HUMAN

PLANETARY

STELLAR

GALACTIC

UNIVERSAL

Turn the page to play another Team Universe game! ➤

Part 2: Size Prize!

Have you ever played the card game "War"? Well, Size Prize works the same way. In this game, size takes the prize!

1 Shuffle the deck. Give half of it to your opponent and keep the other half for yourself. Each of you should keep your cards in a face-down stack.

2 Each player flips over the top card at the same time.

3 Whoever's card comes from the larger size scale wins that round, and the winner takes both cards—the Size Prize! If you played "Place Your Order," you know how to use the colored corners of the cards to tell which scale each card belongs in.

4 If the two cards show objects that are in the *same* scale, each player lays down another card to break the tie. If the size scales are *still* the same, keep laying down cards until the tie is broken. The winner gets all the cards that were laid down in that round!

5 The game continues until one player holds all the cards and is proclaimed the Size-Prize winner!

More from Mission Control

Give the "Size Prize" game a twist: This time play the game so that the card with the *smaller* object wins the Size Prize!

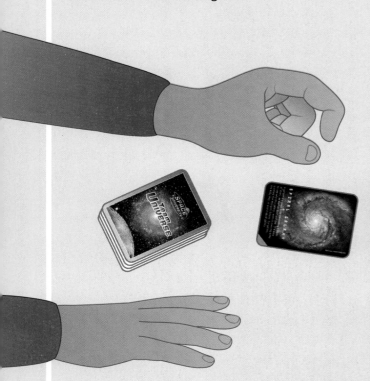

BRAIN-NUMBING NUMBERS

As we hurtle through space, we'll be tossing around a lot of numbers...a lot of HUGE numbers. These numbers are so big that they're often hard to imagine and most of the time our brains just kind of BLEEP over them without stopping to really think about them.

Launch Objective

> Train your brain to contain these gigantic quantities with this quick number intro. It's as easy as one...two...three...trillion!

Your equipment

▶ Just your eyes!

Mission Procedure

1 Here are one hundred stars. Not so hard to handle, right?

2 Below are a *thousand* stars. Still not so bad. There's probably no steam coming out of your ears yet.

3 But can you imagine a *million* (that's 1,000,000) stars? It's harder than you think! But thanks to the Star Counting Society at Space U, you have a head start. Turn the page, and you'll find exactly 20,000 stars. To see a million stars, just imagine 50 of those pages, side by side. Think how much of your wall that would cover!

4 But wait, cadet, if you want to *actually* see a million stars, Mission Control can arrange it! Just blastoff to the Space U web site (www.scholastic.com/space), and there you can feast your eyes on a full supply of one *million* stars!

5 Now that you know what a million stars look like, what's next? Crank up your imagination and think about how a *billion* stars might look. How many sets of a million stars would it take to make a billion stars? You can check your answer on page 48!

ZERO IN!

Hundred	= 100
Thousand	= 1,000
Million	= 1,000,000
Billion	= 1,000,000,000
Trillion	= 1,000,000,000,000

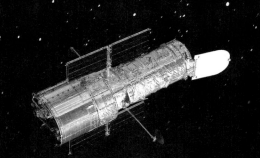

The Hubble Space Telescope has a great view of the universe— it's in orbit around Earth.

Our knowledge of the universe comes from what we can observe, using the tools of science. Some of our most important tools are telescopes, like the ones you see on this page.

What's so great about telescopes? Well, for one thing, you can "telescope" a secret and it won't tell anyone else! But seriously, folks, telescopes are great because they can collect tons more light than the human eye, and they let astronomers see objects that would otherwise be too dim for them to see.

But we've got good news for you, cadet! You don't need to run out and buy a fancy telescope to observe the universe. You can check out the stars of the Milky Way with your naked eyes— just like people have been doing for thousands of years!

This is the kind of telescope people use to look at stars and planets from their backyards.

Picture this!

Past civilizations, like the ancient Greeks, played games of connect-the-dots in the night sky. These people looked up, saw the stars—and decided to create pictures out of them. And that's how constellations were born! This cosmic show includes all sorts of things like reptiles, birds, heroes, ships, goddesses, and monsters. Some of these shapes require a little more imagination than others, as you'll see when you try out the next mission!

CONSTELLATION PR1ZE

Ready for a night of star-studded entertainment? Then make a plan to head outside and see some of the world's most famous constellations for yourself!

Launch Objective

Check out the constellations that are now showing in a sky near you!

Your equipment

- Your eyeballs
- A clear night
- Stargazer's Light Ring **SPACE Case**
- Stargazer's Log or notebook
- Clipboard or another hard surface to write on (optional)
- Pencil

Personnel

- An Intergalactic Adult (IGA)

SPECIAL TRANSMISSION FROM SPACE U: Most of the constellations in this mission can only be spotted in the Northern Hemisphere (that's the half of Earth that's north of the equator and includes places like the United States and Canada). If you're stationed in the Southern Hemisphere, skip ahead to page 26!

Mission Procedure

Part 1: Star Starters

Before you head out to stargaze, you need to prepare:

1 Go to the Space University web site at www.scholastic.com/space and print out your Stargazer's Log. You can use this log to record your "stellar" observations! Or, if you prefer, your own notebook will do just fine.

2 Grab your Stargazer's Light Ring and strap it to your finger. Also grab a pencil and a clipboard if you have one.

3 Join up with an IGA and head outside. Your first stop? The Big Dipper!

Part 2: Spot the Big Dipper!

The Big Dipper is part of the constellation Ursa Major, which means Great Bear. It's made up of seven stars that are pretty easy to spot.

Big Dipper
Ursa Major, the Great Bear

1 To locate the Big Dipper, look to the northern sky. Can you find the four stars that make the dipper's cup, and the three curving stars that make the handle?

2 Depending on the season and the time of night, the Big Dipper will be in a different position—sometimes it looks like it could be holding liquid, and other times it looks like it could be dumping the liquid on you! Make sure to sketch the Big Dipper's position (and note the time of night) in your Stargazer's Log. Use your Stargazer's Light Ring to see as you make your notes.

Big Dipper

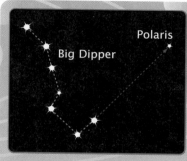

Part 3: Spot Polaris!

Polaris is also known as the North Star. It's not a very bright star, but it's very useful because it shows you which way is...you guessed it...north! Sailors have used it to navigate their ships for centuries. Here's how to use the Big Dipper to find Polaris:

1 Find the two stars that form the end of the cup on the Big Dipper. These stars are known as the pointers. Why? Because they *point* to Polaris!

2 Draw an imaginary line through the two stars and stretch it out across the sky. Go about five times farther than the distance between the two pointer stars, and soon...

3 You'll arrive at Polaris! When you stand facing Polaris, you're looking due north.

Part 4: Spot Cassiopeia!

First, you're probably wondering how to pronounce that mouthful of a name: It's "KASS-ee-oh-PEE-uh." Cassiopeia is a queen—the constellation shows her sitting on her throne. Here's how to find her:

1 Look on the opposite side of Polaris from the Big Dipper.

2 Can you see a W (or an M)? That's Cassiopeia! The center of the W points to Polaris.

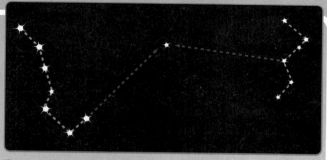

3 Sketch Cassiopeia's position in your Stargazer's Log.

Science, Please!

Because the Earth is constantly on the move, what you see in the night sky changes all the time. As the Earth turns during the night, constellations rise and set, just as the Sun does during the day. As the seasons change, different constellations become visible in the sky. That means you'll never get bored exploring the stars!

Polaris earned its special status as the North Star because it's almost directly above the North Pole. While the other stars appear to move across the sky, Polaris doesn't appear to move at all. It's always above the North Pole, and that means it's always north of you (unless you're hanging out on the North Pole, in which case it'll be right overhead!). The Big Dipper and Cassiopeia revolve around Polaris like they're chasing each other in circles.

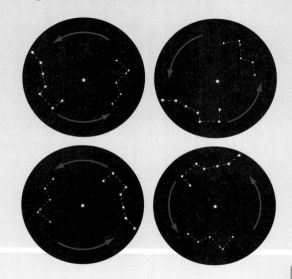

More from Mission Control

1 Your Stargazer's Log will tell you how to use the positions of Cassiopeia and the Big Dipper to tell time!

2 Ready for another stargazing challenge? Then see if you can spot these constellations in the night sky. They're only visible at certain times of the year. Your Stargazer's Log has maps that'll help you figure out where to look. Cadets in the Southern Hemisphere will be able to see these constellations, too!

■ **December to March:** Hunt for **Orion**, the hunter. Remember him from page 12? This guy's kind of flashy, making him one of the most easily spotted constellations. On his arm, you'll discover the star Betelgeuse—a super red-giant star that's about 600 times larger than our Sun!

Orion
Betelgeuse

■ **March to June:** Check out **Leo** the lion— one of the easiest constellations to spot in the spring. See Leo's head? It's formed by stars in the shape of a turned-around question mark. The

Leo
Regulus

dot of this question mark is the extremely bright star Regulus— it's located right where Leo's heart is.

■ **June to September:** Look for **Scorpio**! The heart of this stellar scorpion is the red star Antares. See it? From this famous star, look for Scorpio's long, curving tail.

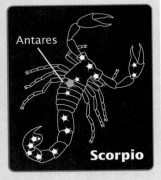

Antares
Scorpio

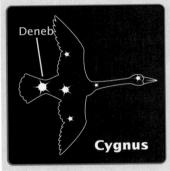

Deneb
Cygnus

■ **September to December:** Search for **Cygnus** the swan. On the tip of the tail of this flying swan, see if you can spot the bright star Deneb.

3 If you spot these constellations, sketch them, and note their locations (and the time) in your Stargazer's Log!

RED LIGHT AT NIGHT, STARGAZER'S DELIGHT!

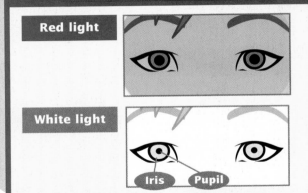

Red light

White light

Iris   Pupil

Why is your Stargazer's Light Ring red? Ask any astronomer, and they'll tell you—it's because red light won't ruin your night vision. Bright white light causes your iris (the colored part of your eye) to close up to protect your pupil (the black circle in the center of your eye). This means your eye takes in less light. With red light, your iris stays wide open, so your eyes can take in the maximum amount of light. That gives you the best view of the stars!

GALAXY QUEST!

Did you know that there are *billions* of galaxies in the observable universe? But besides the Milky Way, there are only three other galaxies that you can see with the naked eye...until now! That's right, cadet, now's your chance to create a new galaxy that you can observe whenever you want!

Launch Objective

Build your own galaxy using glow-in-the-dark stars.

Your equipment

- Glow-in-the-dark stars SPACE Case
- Black construction paper (optional)
- A galactic plan

Personnel

- Possibly an IGA (Intergalactic Adult)

Mission Procedure

1 Before constructing any heavenly body such as a galaxy, it's always a good idea to ask your folks if it's okay. The best place to create your galaxy is on the ceiling of your room, but if that's not okay with your IGAs, you can use black construction paper.

2 Once you have mission clearance, you can take two approaches to your galaxy:

A. Random. Just like the Big Bang sent stars flinging across the universe, you can build your galaxy in a completely free and wild way. Just put stars here and there.

Or...

B. Star plan. Sketch out what you'd like your galaxy to look like. The good thing about this plan is that you can carefully arrange the stars to form constellations. You can make the constellations you learned about on pages 24-26, or you might choose the ones shown below. Or, even better, you can create *new* constellations—of your dog, your mom, your toaster, whatever! If you're using actual constellations, try to pay attention to the colors of stars (that is—if there's a blue star in the constellation, use a blue star sticker!).

3 What's the Intergalactic Adult for? You'll definitely need an adult included on this mission if you have clearance to stick your galaxy on the ceiling above your bed. It can be pretty tricky to reach that far. So just show the IGA where you want the stars placed.

4 When you're finished with your galaxy, turn out the lights and enjoy the view!

Sirius
Adhara
Canis Major, the Big Dog

Pegasus, the Winged Horse

Pollux   Castor
Gemini, the Twins

Light Wave

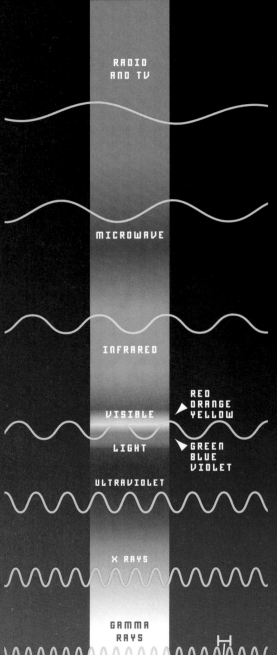

Cadet, a huge part of our understanding of the universe comes from what we know about light.

RADIO
AND TV

MICROWAVE

INFRARED

VISIBLE

RED
ORANGE
YELLOW

LIGHT

GREEN
BLUE
VIOLET

ULTRAVIOLET

X RAYS

GAMMA
RAYS

Wavelength

WHAT IS LIGHT?

Light is electromagnetic radiation, or waves of energy. Light waves travel through space and into your eyes—that's how you see! Water waves have to travel through water to get anywhere, but light waves don't need anything at all. They travel through empty space on their own.

WHAT'S THE MOST IMPORTANT THING ABOUT LIGHT?

Light is the fastest thing in the universe. Albert Einstein, the twentieth-century super-brain, told us that *nothing* can travel faster than light waves. Nothing! Light speed is 186,000 miles (300,000 km) per second—that means light can travel 7.5 times around the Earth in one second!

Light moves fast, but it still takes a *very* long time for it to get across the universe (because the universe is such a big place!). That means if something happens way, way, way out in space (like if a star explodes in a supernova), we won't see it right away. We have to wait for the light to reach us.

IS THERE MORE TO LIGHT THAN THE EYE CAN SEE?

Yes! The chart on the left shows the entire electromagnetic spectrum—or different kinds of light. Our eyes only see a tiny part of this entire spectrum, about 2% of it, called "visible light." We also have the ability to *feel* another kind of light, infrared light, with our skin—we call it "heat."

Night-vision goggles and special cameras can detect infrared light to help people see in the dark. Special space telescopes can also see infrared light, giving us a whole new view of the universe—as the scientist you'll meet on the next page will tell you!

Wavelength is the distance from the top of one wave to the top of the next wave. Different kinds of light have different wavelengths.

Dr. Michelle Thaller
ASTRONOMER

Cadet, say hello to Dr. Michelle Thaller, a NASA astronomer who's working to change the way we see the universe!

Dr. Michelle Thaller works on a NASA mission called SIRTF (pronounced SIR-tiff), which stands for Space Infrared Telescope Facility.

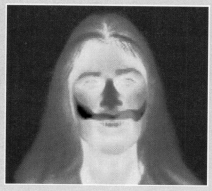

Here's a view of the infrared light (or heat) coming from Dr. Thaller's head! The yellow areas are the hottest, and the purple areas are the coolest. Right before she took the picture, she drew a mustache on her face with an ice cube! Since the ice made her skin cooler, it's visible in infrared.

Question: What kind of work do you do at NASA?

Answer: I work on a new NASA infrared space telescope called SIRTF. I'm an astronomer, but I have a different job than most scientists: I specialize in education. A space telescope isn't much use if no one tells people about its discoveries, so I travel around the country, talking to people, appearing on TV, and generally letting people know about our mission. As an astronomer, I also helped to identify which objects in space SIRTF would look at first.

Q: What does infrared light tell us about the universe that visible light *doesn't* tell us?

A: When you think about it, our eyes are not a great tool for exploring the universe. Everything our eyes can see has to be glowing hot (like a lightbulb or a star), or at least close enough to a light source to be seen in reflected light (like the Moon, which reflects light from the Sun). But there is so much in the universe that doesn't happen to be hot. In infrared light, things that have the temperature of a human body, or even colder, give off their own light.

Q: What kinds of "cool" things will SIRTF help scientists see?

A: Take planets around other stars, for instance. Planets don't give off any visible light of their own, making them nearly impossible to see right up close to their brighter parent stars. But in the infrared, planets give off their own heat, making them easier to detect. We can also see disks of dust around other stars, which is really the leftover material from when planets formed.

Q: What questions will SIRTF help answer?

A: Lots of different ones! We're going to try to find out how common planetary systems are, and how stars themselves are born inside giant dust clouds. We'll also be hunting for giant black holes inside distant galaxies.

Q: What do you see in the future of astronomy?

A: This is such a great time to be an astronomer! We've only just started to detect planets around distant stars, and already we know of over a hundred planets beyond our solar system. In another ten years, I bet we'll find thousands. The future of astronomy looks incredibly bright!

This is SIRTF, a telescope that sees the universe in infrared light. Behind it is a view of the sky in infrared.

WHO TURNED OUT THE LIGHTS?

By now, you probably know that space is one dark place, at least to *our* eyes! But have you ever wondered why space is so dark when it's full of shining stars?

Launch Objective

▶ Discover why space is black.

Your equipment

▶ Stargazer's Light Ring **SPACE Case**
▶ A dark room
▶ Baby powder (flour or cornstarch will also work)

Mission Procedure

1 Strap your Stargazer's Light Ring on your finger and turn it on.

2 Put your other hand in front of the beam of light, about 5 inches from the ring.

3 Check it out: A circle shape will form on your hand, but you probably won't be able to see any light between the ring and your hand. Why?

4 Now it's time to unlock the power of powder—baby powder, that is! Grab a baby powder container and sprinkle a little powder in front of the light. See how the beam of light becomes clearly visible when you spray baby powder into it?

Science, Please!

Cadet, just remember—it's all about reflection. In order for you to see light, it has to bounce off something and get to your eyes. Your hand or the baby powder reflects the light to your eyes, allowing you to see the beam of light. The same is true for space. Beams of starlight travel through space, but since space is almost totally empty, there is nothing to reflect the light for us to see. So space is dark! Get it?

3...2...1...

Now, the moment every Space U cadet has been waiting for...let's fire up the rockets and head into space!

Part 4:
Space Exploration

WHAT IS SPACE EXPLORATION?

Good question, cadet! Space exploration takes place whenever we venture out beyond Earth's atmosphere. This can happen in many different ways—we can fire unmanned probes across the solar system in search of stellar knowledge; we can send remote-control vehicles to roam around another planet; or, most spectacularly, we can actually send *ourselves* out into space!

WHO CAN I TALK TO ABOUT GETTING MYSELF INTO SPACE?

Do you have a few million dollars just lying around your bedroom? Are there a couple hundred rocket scientists hanging out in your living room playing video games? If not, cadet, you might want to check out one of the space agencies described below. It takes a ton of resources and lots (LOTS!) of money to launch Earthlings into space.

NASA

On October 1, 1958, the National Aeronautics and Space Administration was born. More than one Space U cadet has sprained his or her tongue saying this long name, so it's easier—and recommended for tongue safety—to just say NASA. This space agency is all about space exploration and research, and its mission is:

To improve life here,	**to extend life to there,**	**to find life beyond.**
NASA conducts scientific research and develops new inventions that help people on Earth.	NASA makes it possible for people to travel and live in space.	NASA searches for signs of alien life.

NASA has been very busy in the half-century since it was born. In 1969, just eleven years after its birth, NASA put the first Earthlings on the Moon. Then, in 1981, NASA launched its first space shuttle mission. The space shuttle program has delivered satellites, space telescopes, and other equipment into orbit. Shuttles have also brought astronauts and supplies to the International Space Station (ISS)—an orbiting space lab that NASA and several other nations have been building since 1998. For more highlights from NASA's history, check out pages 33–35.

WHAT IF I'M ON VACATION IN ANOTHER COUNTRY AND WANT TO BLAST OFF INTO SPACE?

If you're on vacation in Russia, you're in luck! The Russians maintain one of the largest, most productive space agencies on the planet. After the United States and Russia, the space agency of Europe is the largest. Other countries with growing space programs are Canada, China, Japan, and Israel.

The International Space Station (ISS) in orbit around Earth.

PATCH Me In

Fashion has its place—even in space! All the well-dressed space explorers have cool patches to show off where they've been and what they've been up to in the universe. That's why you'll find a mission patch for your Space U training in your Space Case.

WHAT IS A MISSION PATCH?

Imagine if someone asked you to draw a picture of a space mission.

You'd want to include some symbols that represent the various parts of the mission, right? You'd probably also want to include the names of the people who went on the mission. Well, cadet, that's how mission patches work!

Patched together on these pages are just a few examples from the hundreds of NASA mission patches. Read all about 'em so you can get patched in!

APOLLO 11 MISSION PATCH

This is probably the most famous of all space mission patches. Why? Because in 1969, the *Apollo 11* crew members—including Neil Armstrong—wore this patch when they became the first humans to land on the surface of the Moon! Notice the bald eagle? *Apollo 11*'s lunar lander was called the *Eagle*—plus the bird symbolizes America.

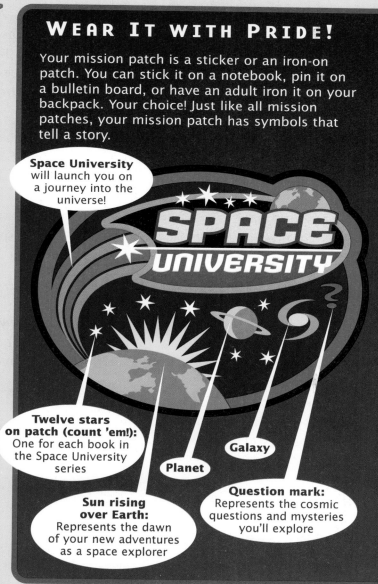

WEAR IT WITH PRIDE!

Your mission patch is a sticker or an iron-on patch. You can stick it on a notebook, pin it on a bulletin board, or have an adult iron it on your backpack. Your choice! Just like all mission patches, your mission patch has symbols that tell a story.

Space University will launch you on a journey into the universe!

Twelve stars on patch (count 'em!): One for each book in the Space University series

Sun rising over Earth: Represents the dawn of your new adventures as a space explorer

Planet

Galaxy

Question mark: Represents the cosmic questions and mysteries you'll explore

SKYLAB 2 MISSION PATCH

In the 1970s, a series of missions put an orbiting "Skylab" (an early space station) into outer space. Designed for long missions, *Skylab* proved that humans could live in space for extended periods, and it expanded our knowledge of astronomy. The crew of *Skylab 2* worked on solar astronomy and conducted experiments with resources found on Earth. How are these aspects of the mission shown on the patch?

STS-71 MISSION PATCH

What do you get when you put six Americans and four Russians together in space? You get Space Transportation System Mission #71 (STS-71), that's what! This mission, which took place in 1995, was the first space docking between an American space shuttle and the Russian space station, Mir. When the two spacecraft linked up, together they became the largest craft ever to orbit Earth.

STS-31 MISSION PATCH

This is the space shuttle mission that delivered the Hubble Space Telescope into its orbit around Earth in 1990 (you can see this telescope on page 23). Unfortunately, Hubble had blurry vision, so NASA had to go back and give the telescope a "contact lens" on a later mission! Now Hubble gives us stunning views of distant galaxies and other far-out things!

ISS-5 EXPEDITION PATCH

The International Space Station (ISS) was built by many countries working together (including the U.S., Russia, Canada, and others). This patch, from a June 2002 mission, shows a space shuttle docked to the ISS to deliver a new crew. The American and Russian flags represent the nationalities of the crew members, and the seventeen stars in the background symbolize all of the people who had visited or lived aboard the ISS up to that time.

The names of Russian crew members (in the Russian alphabet).

QuickBlast

Hatch-A-Patch

Cadet, now's your chance to create your own mission patch! Choose your own symbols and name your own crew for the future mission of your choice! To get started, just blast off to the Space U web site at www.scholastic.com/space, and remember to bring your password, which you'll find on Planet Password on page 6.

Patch Match

A — MOHRI KREGEL VOSS KAVANDI THIELE GORIE

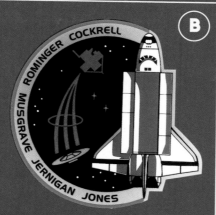

B — ROMINGER COCKRELL MUSGRAVE JERNIGAN JONES

C — RICHARDS CABANA MELNICK SHEPHERD AKERS

D — FERGUSON DAVIS BROWN ROMINGER CURBEAM ROBINSON 85

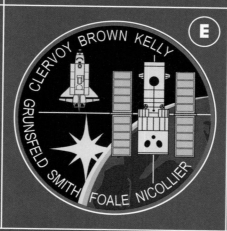

E — CLERVOY BROWN KELLY GRUNSFELD SMITH FOALE NICOLLIER

F — PETTIT БУДАРИН BOWERSOX

Can you match the patch with its mission? Use the symbols to help you decide, and check your answers on page 48!

1. A 1997 space shuttle mission that studied the Earth's atmosphere and tested a Japanese robotic arm designed for use on the International Space Station. The robotic arm is shown inside the shuttle's bay doors.

2. The third space shuttle mission to service and improve the Hubble Space Telescope (in 1999). The patch shows the space shuttle's bay doors open, ready to take in the telescope.

3. A space shuttle mission during 1996, in which two satellites were deployed. The patch has sixteen stars, one star for each day of the mission.

4. The ISS-6 expedition patch from November 2002, showing the ISS in orbit around Earth and the spirit of international teamwork.

5. A space shuttle mission in February 2000 when radar was used to create a three-dimensional map of the Earth.

6. The 1990 space shuttle mission that sent the *Ulysses* satellite on its journey across the solar system toward Jupiter.

FIZZ WIZZ

So the space shuttles at NASA are all booked? And the Russian space agency wants a few million dollars to take you for a ride? Don't worry! Just build your own rocket! Here's how.

Launch Objective

▶ **Build a working rocket.**

Your equipment

▶ **Clear 35mm film container (the Fuji film kind)**
▶ **Plain paper**
▶ **Markers or crayons**
▶ **Scissors**
▶ **Tape**
▶ **Water**
▶ **Half an Alka-Seltzer tablet**

Personnel

▶ **An Intergalactic Adult (IGA)**

Mission Procedure

1 Find an outdoor launch spot and obtain clearance from an Intergalactic Adult. (In other words, let your folks know what you're up to and make sure they're okay with the launch.)

2 The paper will make the "body" of your rocket, so you might want to jazz it up with a colorful design. (Add color, numbers, names—whatever you want!)

3 Roll the paper into a tube around the film container with the open end of the container facing out. Make sure the rim of the container is visible—you have to be able to push the lid back on.

4 Tape the paper tube securely in place.

5 Cut a piece of paper into a circle, cut a slit from the edge of the circle to the center, and shape the circle into a cone. Tape it to the top of the rocket body for a fabulous nose cone.

6 OPTIONAL: Cut out small triangles from another piece of paper and tape them on as rocket fins.

7 Hold the rocket upside down and fill the film container ¼ full of water. Don't put *too* much water inside!

8 Place half an Alka-Seltzer tablet into the container.

9 *Quickly* replace the lid and put the rocket down right side up.

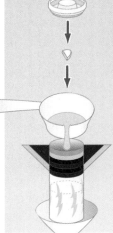

ROCKET

10 Move away! Stand back and start the countdown to liftoff!

Science, Please!

When you mix the Alka Seltzer and water, you're starting a reaction that produces carbon dioxide gas. The gas creates pressure inside the sealed film container that continues to build and build—until there's enough pressure to blow the container free from its lid. That's the moment your rocket launches!

And with that launch, a struggle begins with the force of gravity, which is constantly pulling at the rocket and trying to get it to come back down to Earth. At first, the power of the rocket is able to overcome gravity—but then, of course, the rocket falls to the ground once its fizz is hizz-tory!

FLASH FACT

A rocket is a vehicle that's propelled by stuff that's ejected out of it—like a deflating balloon that zooms around, powered by escaping air.

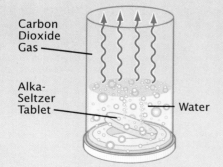

Carbon Dioxide Gas

Alka-Seltzer Tablet

Water

More from Mission Control

The big brains at Mission Control like the rocket you've built...but they wonder if it could be even more powerful. They have a few questions for you:

- Does the water temperature affect the rocket's performance? (Try water a little warmer or cooler.)

- How about changing the amount of water or Alka-Seltzer in the container—does that affect how well the rocket flies?

- Would you get better results if you taped the Alka-Seltzer tablet to the lid?

- Can you design a rocket that is powered by two or three (or maybe even four!) film containers?

Top Tips FROM THE FIZZ WIZZ ROCKET PROS

"This rocket won't work with black film containers with gray lids. Use clear film containers, like the Fuji kind."
–Dr. Philip Mylid

"If you crush the Alka-Seltzer tablets into a powder, you'll speed up the reaction and make your rocket more powerful."
–Prof. Imso Ghassy

"Less water in the container means more power—because that leaves more room for gas to build up."
–Commander Hugh B. Dryer

ASTRONAUT Jerry Ross

Say hello to Colonel Jerry Ross, a real-life astronaut and the first human to be launched into space seven times! Colonel Ross has spent over 1,393 hours (about 58 days) in space, and holds U.S. records for most space walks (nine) and most space-walking time (58 hours and 18 minutes). Space U caught up with Col. Ross at the Johnson Space Center in Houston, Texas.

Question: What's liftoff like?

Answer: That's by far the most exciting part of the ride, no doubt. You're in a seat on your back and then the solid rocket motors ignite! That's a real kick in the pants! Boom! You really feel the awesome power that's being released about 100 feet behind you!

Q: What normal action feels the most different when you're in space?

A: In space, you can't set something down and expect it to stay there. It will float away! Normally, we use little patches of Velcro so that hardware or food containers will stick to places.

Q: What do you do with your free time in space?

A: I like to listen to music and look out the window at the world floating below. But there's very little free time—we have 16-hour workdays and 8-hour sleep periods.

Q: What feeling on Earth is like being in space?

A: Floating around in a swimming pool. Except up there, you don't have to hold your breath, you don't get wet, and you don't have to swim. If you want to go somewhere, you just push off and float there.

Q: Is it hard to readjust to Earth's gravity?

A: For the first hour or so, you feel like there's this gorilla on your shoulders. It's just normal gravity, but because you've been out of it for a while, it feels awful heavy.

Q: Where will our Space U cadets go in space?

A: Within the next fifty years, there's a chance people will go to Mars, walk on it, maybe live there, and return to Earth.

Q: Thanks, Colonel Ross! You rock-et!

Here's Col. Ross on a space walk— or an EVA (extravehicular activity) as NASA calls it. He's installing new features on the International Space Station. To keep him rooted in place while he works, his feet are anchored to the Space Station's "Canadarm," a robotic arm, built in Canada, that can serve as a moving work platform.

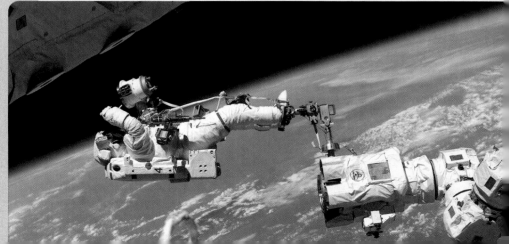

Take a SPACE HIKE!

All right, cadet! It's time for the ultimate space experience! We're going to leave the spacecraft and go for a little EVA (extravehicular activity). VERY IMPORTANT: Whatever you do...do not head out into space without your space suit!

What would happen to someone in space without a space suit?

WINDED!

Space doesn't have any air. That means it doesn't have the *air pressure* we're used to here on Earth (Really! Air *presses* on us—try the next mission if you don't believe it!). Anyway, without air pressure, the air inside your lungs would be free to rush out into space. Gases in your body would expand and make your body blow up like a balloon. Your blood would get all bubbly (because there are gases dissolved in it), and it wouldn't be able to do its job. Basically, you'd swell up and be unconscious in under fifteen seconds. Doesn't sound like a very fun experience, huh?

FROZEN AND BAKED!

And that's not the worst of it. Say that you somehow survived the lack of air pressure... you'd still have to deal with the wild temperature extremes that can range from 120 degrees Celsius (248° F) in sunlight to minus 100 degrees Celsius (-148° F) in a shaded area.

WHAPPED!

Oh! And watch out for flying objects! Because there's no air in space, there's nothing to slow stuff down (like wind resistance slows down airplanes). Tiny meteoroids fly through space so fast that they can easily penetrate human skin! And the junk left behind by other space missions (like paint chips and bits of metal from rockets) is just as dangerous. Fortunately, space is a really huge and mostly empty place, so you're not likely to encounter any of this stuff. But still, you have to be careful!

Space suits keep astronauts safe from the dangers of the space environment.

SPACE

You've probably heard that space is a *vacuum*. (No, it won't help out by cleaning up around the house—a "vacuum" is just another way of saying there's no air out there!). What can a vacuum like space do to a space explorer's everyday belongings? Better find out now before you take off!

Launch Objective

> **Discover the amazing things that the space environment can do to ordinary objects.**

Your equipment

- **Space Simulator**
  SPACE Case
- **Large marshmallow (very fresh)**
- **Small balloon**
- **Glob of shaving cream**

Mission Procedure

1 Choose an object for the mission. What will be the lucky item? The marshmallow, the balloon, or the glob of shaving cream? Try all three if you want (just not all at once!).

2 Pop the object into the Simulator. If you're using the balloon, blow it up very slightly—just get a little air into it—and tie it before you put it in the Simulator. For the shaving cream, just squirt a small glob into the Simulator. For the marshmallow, just toss one inside!

3 Screw on the lid.

4 Place the rubber stopper in the hole in the lid. Press it in firmly.

5 Place the pump on top of the stopper and start pumping the air out of the container. This shouldn't take long, maybe ten seconds.

6 Watch the object expand! This is what would happen to the object if it got tossed out into space!

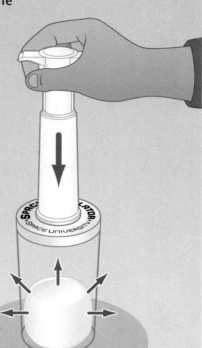

SIMULATOR

7 Let the air back into the container by squeezing the sides of the stopper (put your fingers where it says PRESS). What happens to the object?

HISSS!

Science, Please!

Your Space Simulator pump removes *some* of the air from the container—not all of it. To create a true vacuum, you'd need some very special equipment. With less air putting pressure on the objects, they're able to expand into the space around them. When you open the Simulator's valve, air rushes back inside and the objects must once again deal with normal air pressure. That means they'll shrink back down to normal size (or smaller in the case of the marshmallow, because it loses its flexibility and support when it gets stretched!).

More from Mission Control

You know how we told you that your blood would become "bubbly" if you went out into space without a protective suit? Well, now we want to *show* you—using soda, not blood, of course!

1 Pour a little soda into the Simulator. Let it sit for a few minutes until the bubbles stop fizzing.

2 Now put the lid on the Simulator and start pumping air out.

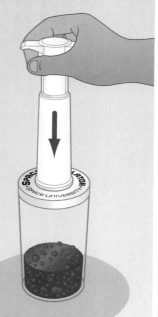

3 What happens to the soda? The soda has gas dissolved in it—and the gas expands and bubbles when the air is removed. The same thing would happen to your blood if you went out into space without a space suit!

What are the most mysterious mysteries of space? Well, first things first...

IS THERE LIFE OUT THERE?

Cadet, are you expecting little green men to park their flying saucer in your backyard? Or maybe you're expecting to see a twelve-headed Ghwoznik from the planet Thedra cruise by in its Earth lander? Sure, those things *might* happen....

But scientists think you have a better chance of finding something like green *ooze* rather than green men. The search for life in the universe isn't always about finding "intelligent" life—creatures that have evolved to the point where they can communicate with Earthlings. The cosmic search for the living includes all kinds of life, even the microscopic. Space explorers will probably come across tiny signs of life—like one-celled organisms—before they encounter any three-legged creatures. But, cadet, you never know....

MEET YOUR NEIGHBORS!

Okay, so other life in the universe has yet to be discovered. But that doesn't mean you have to wait to imagine your cosmic neighbors! We've created a few creatures to inspire you in your search for life. After you've met the aliens on these pages, see if you can create a few of your own!

GALAOZZIAN from Planet Inottem
- Three eyes can detect many kinds of light.
- One leg is similar to a bouncy spring.
- When it's scared, it becomes see-through.

PUFFROR from Planet Squamex
- Floats in swamps.
- Shoots up flames to cook flying prey.

ANOMLA from Planet Alliyew
- Never fully asleep; one of its three heads is always awake.
- Digs through snow using its nose like a shovel.

CHILLYWORMS from Planet Iko
- Burrow through ice with their razor-sharp teeth.
- No eyes.

GLASTLES from Planet Yoik
- Crystal-like bodies with super-sharp edges.
- Try very hard to be stepped on so they can feed on blood from cut feet.

OCUROCKERS from Planet Quimjon
- Grow on rocks.
- Form communities by sending out tendrils.

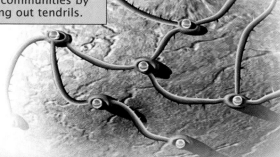

TONGLIDER from Planet Zizzle
- Has metallic skin to reflect intense sunlight.
- Has eyes underneath its wings to spot prey.
- Spears prey with forked tail.

SPONRICETTE from Planet Nansu Yelonnoc
- Must never leave the water, even for a moment.
- Decorations on gills are a sign of wealth.
- Two tails (one in front, the other in back) spin like propellers.

QuickBlast

Create your own alien!

Okay, cadet, are your creative juices flowing? Then whip up your own alien and send your creation to Space University Mission Control at the address below. Be sure to include your alien's name, its home planet, and some descriptions of its most out-of-this-world features! We'll post as many aliens as we can to the Space University web site bulletin board.

TO:
Space University Mission Control
557 Broadway, 10th Floor
New York, New York 10012

How far can we travel in the
UNIVERSE?

Well, cadet, it depends how much time you have. Do you have a *lot* of time on your hands? If so, you could hitch a ride on a space probe like *Voyager* (which you can read about on the next page) to a star system called Alpha Centauri, Earth's closest stellar neighbor. Alpha Centauri might have its own planets that could support life—so your trip might really pay off. It's only about 40 trillion (that's 40,000,000,000,000) kilometers away, and it would only take you about 80,000 years to get there!

Too long? Okay, imagine that you've skipped the relatively slow space probe and are traveling in a spacecraft that uses the most current technology. The trip would only take 10,000 years. Is that better?

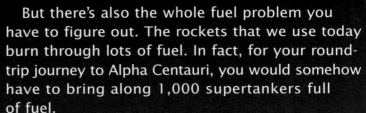

But there's also the whole fuel problem you have to figure out. The rockets that we use today burn through lots of fuel. In fact, for your round-trip journey to Alpha Centauri, you would somehow have to bring along 1,000 supertankers full of fuel.

Then, of course, there's always the speed limit issue. According to our old pal Albert Einstein, nothing can travel faster than the speed of light. That's pretty fast (see "Light the Way!" on page 28), but this speed limit puts some constraints on where we can travel in the universe. And as far as we know right now, nothing with mass (that's you) can even travel at the speed of light anyway.

WHAT'S NEXT?

In future missions, you'll be checking out new kinds of space transportation that might someday make a trip to Alpha Centauri a reality. These include new kinds of spacecraft engines, and even routes through worm holes (these are double-ended black holes— very cool!).

QuickBlast

Alpha Bet!

If one of today's spacecraft could make the trip to Alpha Centauri in about 10,000 years, how long do you think it would take *light* to make the trip?

A) 4 seconds   B) 4 months   C) 4 years

Check your answer on page 48!

PROBE the Universe!

While it's definitely exciting for people to venture out into space, we don't *have* to explore the universe that way. We can send out probes—spacecraft without people on board—to go where no human can currently go. These probes become our eyes and ears as they explore faraway places.

BON VOYAGER!

NASA has been sending out probes for decades. In 1977, NASA sent the *Voyager* probes (*Voyager 1* and *Voyager 2*) on a grand tour of the outer solar system. These probes beamed images and scientific data back to Earth as they zoomed past Jupiter, Saturn, Uranus, and Neptune—and now they've left our solar system and are zooming into deep space!

The probe *Voyager 1* has scored the ultimate out-of-this-world record: It's gone farther than any human-made object has ever gone before!

ROVING ON THE RED PLANET

While no human has set foot there yet, Earth has sent *lots* of probes and landers to check out Mars. This makes Mars one of the most explored planets in the solar system! Sure, it's a cold, dusty planet, but there's evidence that Mars wasn't always that way. In 1997, NASA's *Pathfinder* mission found that some rocks on Mars had been pushed and shoved into place by a huge flood that happened about two billion years ago.

NASA's *Pathfinder* lander carried a tiny robotic vehicle (a "rover") called *Sojourner*. With help from *Sojourner*'s camera and laser, remote controllers on Earth drove *Sojourner* around the landing area, studying Martian rocks.

Sojourner

Pathfinder

when can we live on the MOON?

Can you wait about fifty years? That's the time some say it will take for us to build permanent bases on the Moon. What could you do in your new home on the Moon? Check out this page for a bunch of ideas:

Talk to Earth
Communication dishes send and receive messages.

Count the Stars
The far side of the Moon is a great spot for stargazing. Colonists will want to set up a telescope there!

Build a Nest
Homes on the Moon may be built beneath the soil to protect lunar citizens from extreme temperatures and radiation. The Moon lacks an atmosphere, so light from the Sun doesn't filter through anything. That means unprotected lunar citizens will get the full force of the Sun shining on them during the day—that can cause massive sunburn and blindness!

See the Sites
Tourists will probably use the Moon colony as an exotic getaway.

Take a Space Stroll
Special suits make moonwalks possible.

Go for a Ride
Moonmobiles will cruise around the surface.

Gotta Rocket
The Moon colony will offer a great rest stop for space explorers heading farther out into the universe.

Power Up
Solar panels collect the Sun's energy to provide electricity.

Enter a BLACK HOLE!

A black hole is one of the weirdest and wildest things in the universe!

When a large star explodes as a supernova, what's left of it can shrink down very quickly to almost nothing. What remains is a very tiny point in space that has enormous gravity. In fact, the gravity is so great that nothing—not even light—can escape! This is what we call a black hole.

We can't see black holes directly because they don't allow the light around them to get away. That means that the light can't escape to bring the images to our eyes or to our telescopes. But we *do* get to see the light that comes from stuff falling into a black hole, which is called an accretion disk. It looks kind of like the spinning water going down the drain after you take a bath.

Accretion disk

QuickBlast

Spaghetti Kid

Gravity in a black hole is so strong that, if you started to enter one, the gravity would grab onto your toe and pull your body until it was stretched out in a very long, thin line. Some scientists called this process "spaghettification" (really!). Here's a fast way to see what you might look like if you fell into a black hole!

1 Draw your picture on a thick rubber band.

2 Stretch out the rubber band slowly. What happens to your picture? This is kind of what you would look like if you fell into a black hole. There's a "hole" lot of stretching going on!

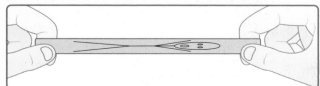

Give Me More SPACE!

Congratulations, cadet, you've arrived at the end of your first course at Space U! Were all of your missions successful ones?

You learned a thing or two that every space explorer should know—like how to launch your own rocket, how to find your way around the night sky, and what it might be like to fall into a black hole.

But wait, cadet! There's so much more where all that came from!

Space U Mission Control will be firing off new books (and new spacey gadgets!) to you every month for the entire time you're enrolled in this cosmically cool space program. Just check out the mission patches on the right to see what kinds of topics Space U has in store for you. So, keep your head in the stars and your eye on your mailbox, because the countdown to your next space adventure starts...now!

FUTURE SPACE U BOOKS INCLUDE:

Space Travel

Amazing Astronomy

Earth's Neighborhood

Stars and Galaxies

The Search for Life in the Universe

Science in Orbit

Exploring Other Worlds

Mars: Roving on the Red Planet

Living on the International Space Station

Great Cosmic Questions

THE ANSWER STATION

Page 12, Star Search! See image below. (A) Orion, (B) Andromeda Galaxy, (C) Large Magellanic Cloud, (D) Small Magellanic Cloud

Page 14, Mark Your Calendar!
The Sun's birthday is August 30.
The Earth was formed over the next 2–3 days.

Page 19, Size 'Em Up!
Part 1: Look at the bottom right corner of each card. Each scale has a different color. Atomic is red; human is orange; planetary is yellow; stellar is green; galactic is blue; and universal is purple. If you have everything arranged correctly, the cards should be in rainbow order!

Page 21, Brain-Numbing Numbers
5) It would take 1,000 sets of a million stars to make a billion stars.

Page 35, Patch Match
1) D   2) E   3) B   4) F   5) A   6) C

Page 44, Alpha Bet!
C) 4 years